Handwriting Practice Books for Adults

CHILDREN'S READING & WRITING EDUCATION BOOKS

All Rights reserved. No part of this book may be reproduced or used in any way or form or by any means whether electronic or mechanical, this means that you cannot record or photocopy any material ideas or tips that are provided in this book

Copyright 2016

Trace and rewrite the famous quotes.

The artist is nothing without the gift, but the gift is nothing without work.

—Emile Zola

There is more stupidity than hydrogen in the universe, and it has a longer shelf life.
—Frank Zappa

The richest man is
not he who has the
most, but he who
needs the least.
—Unknown Author

You must be the change you wish to see in the world.
— Mahatma Gandhi

The most difficult thing is the decision to act, the rest is merely tenacity.
— Amelia Earhart

Always forgive your enemies; nothing annoys them so much.

—Oscar Wilde

> Life isn't about getting and having, it's about giving and being.
> —Kevin Kruse

Life is 10% what happens to me and 90% of how I react to it.
—Charles Swindoll

The best time to plant a tree was 20 years ago. The second best time is now.
—Chinese Proverb

Believe those who are seeking the truth. Doubt those who find it.

—André Gide

A dog is the only thing on earth that loves you more than he loves himself.
— Josh Billings

Dogs are not our whole life, but they make our lives whole.

—Roger Caras

Your time is limited, so don't waste it living someone else's life.
— Steve Jobs

I am not a product
of my circumstances.
I am a product of
my decisions.
—Stephen Covey

Every child is an artist.
The problem is how
to remain an artist
once he grows up.
—Pablo Picasso

Whether you think you can or you think you can't, you're right.
—Henry Ford

Advice is what we ask for when we already know the answer but wish we didn't.

—Erica Jong

The trouble with the rat race is that even if you win, you're still a rat.
—Lily Tomlin

Dogs are better than human beings because they know but do not tell.
—Emily Dickinson

I'd rather live with
a good question than
a bad answer.
—Aryeh Frimer

Life shrinks or expands in proportion to one's courage.

—Anaïs Nin

> To love oneself is the beginning of a lifelong romance.
> —Oscar Wilde

Education is a progressive discovery of our own ignorance.
—Will Durant

If everything seems under control, you're just not going fast enough.
—Mario Andretti

The only person you are destined to become is the person you decide to be.
—Ralph Waldo Emerson

Believe you can and you're halfway there.
— Theodore Roosevelt

Obstacles are those frightful things you see when you take your eyes off your goal.

—Henry Ford

Start where you are.
Use what you have.
Do what you can.
—Arthur Ashe

Fall seven times and stand up eight.
—Japanese Proverb

If you want to
lift yourself up,
lift up someone else.
 —Booker T. Washington

It is never too late
to be what you
might have been.
— George Eliot

If you don't build your dream, someone else will hire you to help them build theirs.
—Dhirubhai Ambani

Whenever you find yourself on the side of the majority, it is time to pause and reflect.
— Mark Twain

Great minds discuss ideas; average minds discuss events; small minds discuss people.
—Eleanor Roosevelt

Live as if you were
to die tomorrow.
Learn as if you were
to live forever.
—Mahatma Gandhi

It is our choices,
that show what we
truly are, far more
than our abilities.
— J. K Rowling

www.ingramcontent.com/pod-product-compliance
Lightning Source LLC
LaVergne TN
LVHW061323060426
835507LV00019B/2270